Psalm 91:1-16 NIV

Whoever dwells in the shelter of the Most High will rest in the shadow of the Almighty.

I will say of the Lord, "He is my refuge and my fortress, my God, in whom I trust."

Surely he will save you from the fowler's snare and from the deadly pestilence.

He will cover you with his feathers, and under his wings you will find refuge; his faithfulness will be your shield and rampart.

You will not fear the terror of night, nor the arrow that flies by day, nor the pestilence that stalks in the darkness, nor the plague that destroys at midday.

A thousand may fall at your side, ten thousand at your right hand, but it will not come near you.

You will only observe with your eyes and see the punishment of the wicked.

If you say, "The Lord is my refuge," and you make the Most High your dwelling, no harm will overtake you, no disaster will come near your tent.

For he will command his angels concerning you to guard you in all your ways; they will lift you up in their hands, so that you will not strike your foot against a stone.

You will tread on the lion and the cobra; you will trample the great lion and the serpent.

Because he loves me," says the Lord, "I will rescue him; I will protect him, for he acknowledges my name.

He will call on me, and I will answer him; I will be with him in trouble, I will deliver him and honor him.

With long life I will satisfy him and show him my salvation."

Angels are Coming
An Answer To a Prayer

If we ask anything according to His will, He hears us. John - 16:23

TOMIE GOMEZ

Angels are Coming
Copyright © 2021 by Tomie Gomez. All rights reserved.

No part of this publication may be reproduced, stored in a retrieval system or transmitted in any way by any means, electronic, mechanical, photocopy, recording or otherwise without the prior permission of the author except as provided by USA copyright law.

The opinions expressed by the author are not necessarily those of URLink Print and Media.

1603 Capitol Ave., Suite 310 Cheyenne, Wyoming USA 82001
1-888-980-6523 | admin@urlinkpublishing.com

URLink Print and Media is committed to excellence in the publishing industry.

Book design copyright © 2021 by URLink Print and Media. All rights reserved.

Published in the United States of America
Library of Congress Control Number: 2020923332
ISBN 978-1-64753-562-9 (Paperback)
ISBN 978-1-64753-563-6 (Digital)

11.11.20

*If I have the gift of prophecy and know all
mysteries and all knowledge and if have all
faith so as to remove mountains but
not have love, I am nothing.*

1 Corinthians 13:12 NAB Version

*But now faith, hope, love abide these three;
but the greatest of these is love.*

1 Corinthians 13:13 ESB Version

> "And I Daniel, alone saw the vision, for the men who were with me did not see the vision, but a great trembling fell upon them, and they fled to hide." Daniel 10:7 (ESV)

The Ten Commandments

KJBV Exodus 20:3-17

- *Thou shall have no other gods before me*
- *Thou shalt not make unto thee any graven image*
- *Thou shalt not take the name of the Lord thy God in vain*
- *Remember the Sabbath day, to keep it holy*
- *Honor thy father and thy mother*
- *Thou shalt not kill*
- *Thou shalt not commit adultery*
- *Thou shalt not steal*
- *Thou shalt not bear false witness against thy neighbor*
- *Thou shalt not covet neighbor*

> *1 John 2:3 KJV*
> *And hereby we do know him, if we keep his ten commandments...*

About The Author

"For those who believe in God and love him with all the strength of their heart, body, and mind, each new challenge is an opportunity to communicate with Him, believing that no matter how difficult that trial might be, he is the only one with the power to do the impossible."

I am very thankful my Father God listens to my prayers and has always been with during difficult times.

I was born in Puerto Rico and after traveling for many years, I was finally established in California. It was here in California where I received the visit of identical angels, an experience beyond your imagination.

As a single parent, I learned to live with constant challenges, which I overcame because of my faith in God. In my prayers, I would ask Him to send me angels that would help me with my daily trials. Now that I am retired, I have continued praying, always asking God to send me angels. I enjoy praying under the stars and love to take photos of my Father God's awesome creation.

I have written this book for the honor and glory of God and to let people know that angels are real because I saw them.

> "See, I am sending an angel before you, to guard you on the way and bring you to the place I have prepared"
>
> **Exodus 23:20**

> "This is the confidence we have in approaching God: That if we ask anything according to his will, he hears us, And if we know that he hears us .....whatever we ask-we know that we have what we ask of him".
>
> 1 John 5:14-15 (NIV)

> "See, I am sending an angel ahead of you to guard you along the way and to bring you to the place I have prepared".
>
> Exodus 23:20 (NIV)

Dedication

I dedicate this book to my Father God for the love, strength, and wisdom he is giving me while writing this book; to the angels that one day visited me in my home; and to each person reading this book, believing in God Almighty and His creation.

*and Jacob went on his way and
the angels of God met him.*

Genesis 32:1

> "First of all, then I urge that supplications,
> prayers, intercessions and thanksgiving be made for
> all people, for kings and all who are in high positions,
> that we may live a peaceful and quite life godly and
> dignified in every way" This is good and it is pleasing
> in the sight of God our savior, who desires all people to
> be saved and to come to the knowledge of the truth"
>
> 1 Timothy 2-4 (ESV)

My Prayer

Open my eyes, oh Lord, that I can see your creation
Open my ears, Oh Lord that I can hear your word
Open my heart, oh Lord, so that I can show your love
Open my lips, oh Lord, so that I can speak the truth
My Father God, I pray today
Teach me to think before I speak
Give me words that come from thee so I don't hurt a human being
Show me the road to get to you
The narrow one will lift me up
Help me to live a humble life
Sharing your blessings and treating others like Jesus did
And for my children, I ask you, God, to please send angels
That will protect them, keeping them safe and in your hands,
Father in heaven, I'm getting old, I know one day I must go home

But what I planted will grow and grow
Today I pray, my Father God
To touch each seed I planted, Lord, to bless the land where they will grow
Letting them shine like stars above
So when I go passing the sun, the ones behind can sow their crop
Then I can say I did my part, I helped this world planting the seeds with faith and love
No more sadness, worries are gone I am with God, I made it home

By Tomie Gomez

> Genesis 19:1 and there came two angels to Sodom at even; and Lot sat in the gate of Sodom: and Lot seeing them rose up to meet them; and he bowed himself with his face toward the ground;
>
> Genesis 19:1 (KJV)

Preface

"Then the angel I saw standing on the sea and on the land raised his right hand to heaven"
Rev- 10:5 New International Bible

I Want to thank you, Father God, for sending angels to my home when I was least expecting them and for giving me the opportunity to see how angels in heaven are. Even though I don't consider myself worthy of receiving this magnificent gift, I praise you and thank you, Father God, for giving me a vision that has changed my life. I also thank you, God Almighty, for the health and strength you have given me, which has made it possible for me to write and share this experience with others.

When I started writing this book, I wasn't sure if I was going to be able to continue writing or even publish it, considering it was going to be a big project that was going to require time and ability to write a true story that would touch people the way it has touched me. Also, I wasn't sure if this vision was to be told through a written book or just to family and friends who know me better. Not having an idea as to where to begin with the production of this book, I started to pray—asking God for direction, putting him first like I always do when making a decision.

I began asking God to show me and lead my steps if this book was to be written for his honor and glory.

One day, I contacted the publishing company and talked to a representative, who asked me a few questions regarding the book. After a long talk about my experience, I noticed that the representative had been touched by our conversation; at that moment, I felt a strong desire to continue writing the book, asking God through prayer for words of knowledge and wisdom. For me, the biggest challenge was going to be typing the story because typing has never been one of my strengths. When I told a good friend that it was going to be a struggle typing my story, I saw God's hand move; to my surprise, she said she would do the typing for me. Like a faithful friend, she has been here by my side—typing the story and being amazed by my experiences. I have asked my family, friends, and people of faith to pray for me while writing this book; I want to thank each one of you, and I ask God to bless you in a special way for the support you have given me through all your prayers.

Before I start telling you about the apparition of angels in my son's room, I consider the following recount of some events in my life to be very important, as I believe things are connected—creating a purpose and reason for each minute and second in our life. I also believe that with faith and prayers, we can change negative into positive and receive what we ask from God if what we are asking for is part of his plan. It is difficult to talk about my personal life, but by telling you the most important events, I hope you can find a connection between my life and the encounter with angels or at least find a message that would show you how putting God first in our lives is like having a celestial key unlocking doors on earth, changing one's pain and confusion to peace and hope. It would be an extraordinary moment for me to hear that a single parent, an educator, a family struggling with trials, or any other person on this planet was touched in a special way while reading this book.

> *"With all my heart I praise you, Lord In the presence of angels, I sing your praises."* Psalm 138:1 Contemporary English Version

A life with challenges

I was born in Puerto Rico and raised in Yabucoa—a small town known for its sugarcane and for the beautiful beach of Santa Lucia, which is fifteen minutes away from my parents' home. With my parents, I learned the importance of a good education and to put God first in everything I do. I have always lived a simple life, but at the same time a life full of challenges, which I've overcome because of my faith in God and my desire to succeed in life. While finishing my bachelor's degree at the University of Puerto Rico, I got married and had my first child. When he was a year old, I moved to Miami, Florida with my husband. Miami was a good place to start, with nice weather and friendly people I enjoyed talking to while having a delicious cup of coffee, which is one of my favorite things to do. After a few months in Miami, my brother-in-law and his family moved to Bridgeport, Connecticut. We followed them there, and that's where we would start a new life. As a young couple, we didn't have much in terms of material things, but I was happy and ready for a new challenge—moving toward success in my life. I knew it was going to be difficult for me to succeed but knowing that everything is possible if we pray to our Father God, having faith in him, I kept trying to

> **Genesis 19:15 and when the morning arose, then the angels hastened Lot, saying, Arise, take thy wife, and thy two daughters, which are here; lest thou be consumed in the iniquity of the city.**

find my place in the new community while waiting for God to do his will. In the meantime, I worked very hard to complete the necessary steps that would lead me to accomplish my goals in life.

God gave me a very special blessing almost immediately when I got my first job as a teacher helping high school students return to school. It was a big challenge to teach some of these students because I was quite young, and the lessons taught were not the only task I had to deal with in my classroom. I had to start by changing the mentality and attitude some of my students had toward their education so that I could teach them the subjects I handled as part of their curriculum. I worked very hard that year because I wanted to make a difference in their lives. I always taught my students with honesty and respect, while expecting the same from them. I was thankful to my Father God for the change I noticed in my students' attitude toward the end of the school year. I knew that by promoting their self-esteem, I was also promoting good attitude, which comes with positive words of encouragement while stressing honesty, respect, and love on a daily basis.

That experience led me to a first-grade teaching position in a public school the following year. While teaching I started working on my Master's Degree in counseling needed to complete a second credential. Two years later, God blessed me with a second job as a part time counselor for a community college, expanding my portfolio of experiences and increasing my income. This part time job was very rewarding because while helping the students with classes and schedules, I was also there for them when they needed counseling or help with other concerns affecting their education. We became a close family, and I was looking forward to a full-time position at the college.

> **Genesis 28:12 and he dreamed, and behold a ladder set up on the earth, and the top of it reached to heaven: and behold the angels of God ascending and descending on it.**

My life was full of new challenges; but with a healthy body and a strong mind, I was ready to successfully complete each task required with a strong mind I was ready to successfully complete each task required from me, always remembering that God is in the midst of everything I do. One day while waiting for my freshmen students in my office, one of the students who had attended my class for high school came to see me and let me know she was ready to start taking college courses the following year. I thanked the Lord for the wisdom and strength he gave me to teach a challenging class as my first teaching experience and for his gifts of patience, knowledge, and love, which were necessary to make a difference in each one of my students. In 1976, God decided to expand my family and I was thrilled when I found out I was expecting a second baby. When friends told me that I was going to have a baby boy, I started to pray for a daughter since I already had a son. For nine months, I prayed and waited for God's will.

While gently touching my stomach at least once a day, I would talk to my Father God. "Please, Lord, give me a little girl, and I promise you she will serve you for the rest of her life." This was a big promise to God, especially if I was going to depend on my daughter's faith to keep

this promise. When I saw my baby girl at the hospital, I knew God had answered my prayer and I had to be ready to keep my promise, for he had given me the desires of my heart. God had answered my prayer and had shown me that His was the final decision.

Based on the biblical words in **Proverbs 22:6, *"Train a child in the way he should go, and when he is old he will not turn from it,"*** I did my part in instructing both of my children to serve God with all the strength of their hearts and to do what is right according to the scriptures.

> "Bless the Lord, all you angels, mighty in strength and attentive, Obedient to every command."
>
> Psam 103:20

Today, when I see my daughter and her family serving God with all their hearts, always putting him first in their lives, I thank my father in heaven for helping me keep the promise I made Him one day.

Soon after giving birth to my daughter, I started experiencing severe back pain due to a spinal injection while giving birth to my daughter. It became more difficult for me to accomplish my daily tasks as a mother and as a professional. Even though I would start my day in pain, I would not allow it to take control of my body and mind; instead, I saw it as a trial in putting my faith in God who gives us the strength and confidence to go on in life, accepting the things we cannot change. When sickness comes to our life, it can become an obstacle or it can be used to open a heavenly door; giving us an opportunity to better communicate with God, believing everything is possible through his son, Jesus Christ, and because of his wounds we are healed. By concentrating on my job and family, I would not allow any pain or illness to interrupt my responsibilities at the jobs I had been paid to do or my daily activities with the my family God had given me because of his love. The pain continued for almost eighteen years; but I never stopped praying, believing that it was a trial, for God had given me so many blessings.

As you continue reading, you will find out how the pain, which I called "my trial" was relieved from my body in God's time and because of that I say, "God, you are awesome".

With two young children, a new home, and good jobs, I had a prosperous and happy life. I had planned to live in Bridgeport for the rest of my life, enjoying the blessings that my Father God had given us.

When my daughter was a year old, everything suddenly changed in my life and I found myself practically on my own, working and

> "Keep on loving one another as brothers and sisters. Do not forget to show hospitality to strangers, for by so doing some people have shown hospitality to angels without knowing it".
>
> Hebrews 13:1-2 (NIV)

taking care of my two children. My marriage had taken a toll, and I was trying to cope with marital problems I wasn't expecting and certainly wasn't ready to handle at such a young age.

One Christmas Eve after trying to save my marriage without success, while staring at the Christmas tree lights and presents which I had carefully wrapped for my children, I started asking God for a solution to my existing situation and to light my path because I was confused and did not know what to do. It was then I decided to move back to Puerto Rico with my mother, leaving behind everything I had worked so hard for to acquire. I knew I had to start a new life where I had a family I needed for support. This was a very hard decision because even though one should not get attached to material things I needed my car and home for my family.

As we all know, it is very important to purchase airline tickets in advance when traveling during the holidays; but given the fact that I had made a quick decision without much planning, it was going to be difficult to find airline tickets without previous reservations. On the way to the airport, I kept asking God to allow me to find seats on a plane to Puerto Rico that night since we would have to travel on standby. After almost two days on standby at the Kennedy Airport in New York, God touched the heart of a kind pilot. When this pilot saw that I was still there with my children for almost two days, somehow he was able to accommodate us in his flight, and in first class, where some seats were available. I knew God had heard my prayer and was sending us to Puerto Rico in a very special way. Since my flight was at night, and I was sitting by the window, I felt much closer to God and even though I was devastated, I took the opportunity to thank my Father God for all he had given me. Looking at the beautiful sky full of bright stars, I felt his love and knew I was not alone—that he was

> "Do you think I cannot call on my father, and he will at once put at my disposal more than twelve legions of angels"?
>
> Mathew 26:53 (NIV)

going to open doors for me because his love and power over heaven and earth has no limits. Knowing that he was the only one that could help me make the necessary changes in my life that were difficult and painful to make, I would pray by saying, "Dear, God, please take away this pain and bring me joy, happiness, and a new job in Puerto Rico before the month of February to support my children."

I had left Connecticut during Christmas break and knowing that I needed at least a month to find a job, I started looking for employment almost immediately with a strong faith that God had heard my prayer on the plane that night. It was the month of January when I was interviewed and hired as a counselor to start working at the Right to Work Administration in the town of Humacao. God had continued to answer my prayers and had given me a new home with my mother and a new task—helping people in need of employment, which I could very well related to.

As part of my job, I started interviewing people and sending them to training in order to place them in the workforce as soon as possible. It gave me a sense of fulfillment to see my caseload grow as people kept going for training—graduating and getting employed. I still remember the happiness on people's faces when chosen for a job or training in Puerto Rico or the island of Vieques. Flying back to Puerto Rico when I had been scheduled to work in Vieques was a peaceful trip with joy in my heart, for I knew that day I started to reduce the unemployment rate while relieving the stress level of people in need of jobs. Looking through the small window of the plane, I could see the broad blue ocean giving me the appearance of a wide blue screen, where the faces and smiles of people I had helped that day were being projected.

> "For the Lord himself will come down from heaven, with a loud command, with the voice of the archangel and with the trumpet call of God, and the dead in Christ will rise first. After that, we who are still alive and are left will be caught up together with them in the clouds to meet the Lord in the air. And so we will be with the Lord forever."
>
> 1 Thessalonians 4:16-17 (NIV)

Even though I was very happy and successful at my job, not a day would pass I didn't think of the life I had left behind, asking God to help me heal the wounds caused by pain and sadness.

One Sunday night, my sister ,Josie, invited me to visit the Christian church she was attending. It was my first visit to a Christian church, so I took the opportunity to meet new people and keep my sister company during the service that night. When I got out of the car, I could feel the

presence of God in the serene and bright night. A warm breeze complemented the music being played by the church band as the choir of crickets and tiny frogs called "coquis" welcomed the people of God as they entered the temple. I took a few minutes to look around the church, noticing it was packed with people and so was my heart with pains and burdens that I couldn't let go. It had been difficult not to think about my past and to accept my new life in Puerto Rico because even though my mother was very close to me and I had been blessed with a good job, I was still missing my home, students, and friends.

That Sunday night, when the pastor started to preach, my heart was pounding, my legs were weak and wobbly; I felt I was the only person in church with a message that has been preached just for me. While members of the church were singing and praising the Lord, I was sobbing and asking God to change my life and to bring me joy and happiness, which I needed so I could continue with my responsibilities at work and as an exemplary mother to my children.

> "Thinkest thou that I cannot now pray to my Father, and he shall presently give me more than twelve legions of angels"?
>
> Mathew 26:53 (KJV)

That day, I had worn my special blue dress with long sleeves, gathered my hair to the side with a bow, and covered my head with a white veil I borrowed from my sister so I could blend with the women of the congregation without being noticed. Given it was my first time at a Christian church; I couldn't understand what was happening inside me or the purpose for me being there that night. Giving my heart to the Lord, I lifted my hands in prayer asking God Almighty to take away my pain and to show me his way. As I continued praying, I heard the pastor say, "There is a lady here tonight dressed in blue who needs to come to the altar." I looked around and when I saw other women of the congregation dressed in blue, I was sure it wasn't me he was calling to the altar since I was only a visitor and not a member of the congregation. Sitting next to my sister Josie who was in deep prayer, I started feeling what I described to my sister as a strong force pushing me so hard that at the same time I kept pushing my sister without being able to control my body, asking her, "Josie, why have I been pushed?" Her answer was, "Tomie, it's the Holy Spirit." Not wanting to interrupt my sister, I stood up; and as I continued to be pushed, I grabbed my sister's hand, and we both got to the altar. I'll never forget this experience because I got to the altar dragging my feet and not understanding what was happening to me.

The pastor was about seventy years old, and a servant of God admired by his congregation because he was dedicated to his church and served God with all his heart. If he wasn't fasting and praying for a few days at a time in the woods by a river or visiting the sick and those in need in their homes, he was at his church in prayer. He was a man with the gift of prophecy who was always praising the Lord and studying his word. When he touched my head to pray for me that

> "But concerning that day and hour no one knows, not even the angels in heaven ,nor the but Son, but the Father only".
>
> Mathew 24:36

Sunday night, my legs couldn't hold my body; and all I remember is that when I opened my eyes, I knew I had been transformed by the Holy Spirit of God because what I felt and experienced made me a completely different person. It was like I was not the same person who entered the church that night. After this personal encounter with God, I continued serving him and working as a counselor. God had touched me by changing my life and taking away my pain and tears.

The following summer, my children's father came to visit us and asked me to give our marriage a second chance. I consulted with my pastor who, after praying for me, told me not to leave because God was showing him that my decision was not approved by him because the father of my children hadn't changed. Not being mature yet in the Lord and not listening to God's message through my pastor, I went back with my children's father to live in the town of Alamogordo, New Mexico, where he had been stationed because of his new job assignment.

After a month in Alamogordo, I had already organized our apartment, enrolled my son in school, and was ready to start looking for a job as a teacher or counselor when I realized that God had talked to me through my pastor, telling me I had made the wrong decision by moving to New Mexico instead of praying and waiting for his will to be done. My new life wasn't what I expected, and I knew in my heart that Alamogordo was not the place God had chosen for me but the one I chose against his will. Asking my Father God to hear my voice, I began to look at El Paso, Texas newspaper for job opportunities and asking him to help me find a new job and a place to live. After a few days, I found a job opening in the town of San Elizario, Texas, almost two hours away from Alamogordo. A few weeks later, I was crossing the desert between Alamogordo

> "My God sent his angel and shut the lions' mouths, and they have not harmed me, because I was found blameless before him; and also before, you O king, I have done no harm,"
>
> Daniel 6:22 (ESV)

and El Paso, Texas with my two children looking for a town that I have never been to before and a school where I was going to be interviewed for a teaching position. With a strong faith in God and knowing that he is in control of my life, I kept driving and praying for over two hours, admiring the plants of the vast and quiet desert. I noticed that even though they don't get much rain, one can see how the nature touched by God's hand landscaped itself, mixing colorful wildflowers that decorate each side of the road as the majestic cacti stand still providing homes for the many birds that are part of the living desert. I kept driving the long and peaceful road until I found the city of San Elizario and the school where my interview was going to take place that day. I remember San Elizario, as a small and quiet town with maybe one or two stores and a few farm fields where most of the parents of my students worked. I knew my Father God had been in charge that day, guiding my steps and pouring blessings for the well-being of my family.

By the end of the day, I had a job and a furnished apartment including a piano for my children. The following week, I was eager to start working for a wonderful district with people who were kind, hardworking, and willing to help me in every possible way they could. The first lesson was taught to me by some parents who kindly talked about their hard work in the field to provide for their children. I felt welcomed and appreciated as the new teacher for their children, which was very important to me.

My first day of teaching was very special because, as I was learning the name of each student and welcoming the parents, somehow I felt connected to each one of them for one reason or another. My students were very loving, and every day I made sure my high expectations were reflected through my lessons, as I believe

> "For whoever is ashamed of me and of my words in this adulterous and sinful generation of him will the Son of Man also be ashamed when he comes in the glory of his Father with the holy angels."
>
> Mark 8:38 (ESV)

a good education is necessary to be successful in our complex society. It was very important to do my part since I was given all the necessary tools to accomplish my goal—all my students will learn in an environment that is conducive to learning. I always wanted my students to shine like the stars above, as the light in them would shine the path for others. They became part of my extended family, and I was expanding their learning capacities to achieve in all areas of the curriculum, rewarding them with prizes and love. Not having my family close was hard, but that year God sent me two good friends. Both of them loved God with all their hearts, and on weekends we would pray until the early hours of the morning, always asking God to open doors for the three of us and our children. I started visiting their church and sharing my customs and ideas as I learned from them as well. San Elizario was my small paradise.

One of my friends was going to California to visit her family and invited me to come with her—an opportunity that would open new doors for me. We planned our trip in prayer, asking God to guide us in our long trip. We both began the trip to Fresno, California hoping to start a new life in the Golden State. After a few days in Fresno, I decided to apply for a teaching position before going back to Texas, hoping to return for an interview. One day, when I was least expecting it, I was called for a phone interview and to my surprise, I was offered a teaching position the same day. God had opened doors again for my family in a new state and a wonderful school. It was time for Helen and I to start a new life in California, and my Father God had chosen one of his special people on earth-- Helen's brother-in-law, Ruben, to accompany us when moving from El Paso, Texas to California. I knew it was going to be long hours of driving

> Then Elisha prayed and said, "O Lord, please open his eyes that he may see" So the Lord opened the eyes of the young man, and he saw, and behold, the mountain was full of horses and chariots of fire all around Elisha.
>
> 2 Kings 6:37 (ESV)

with children from Texas to Fresno, so I prepared myself with all the necessary items including a big ice chest full of food and began the long journey that took us over two days.

While Ruben drove, and my children entertained themselves in the backseat; my friend and I prayed, talked about our lives, and made plans for when we arrive in California. It was about one o'clock in the morning when we were crossing the Mojave Desert that our car overheated and left us stranded. When Ruben checked the motor, he noticed that the radiator cap was missing and we had no choice but to look for it because it was needed to continue our trip. After looking everywhere and without being able to find it, I started getting worried because we still had a long way to go and had children with us. Asking God for help and with a few survival skills and items in the car, we found a way to feed the children, helping them feel more comfortable under the existing circumstances. While Ruben tried to repair the car, we worked together as a team—one of us was up in prayer and watching while the other one slept. About five o'clock in the morning we got together in a powerful prayer; and when my friend Helen opened the driver's door and looked down, there was the radiator cap by the car. We knew that God had heard our prayer and had given us the place to look and find the missing part needed to continue our trip. Ruben did the best he could to start the car and drove it to the closest gas station. We thanked our Father God for helping us find the missing part and for giving us Ruben as one of his blessings to accompany us on our trip. The following night we were still in the car waiting for the mechanic to finish repairing our car but with a strong faith that God was leading us. During the day while waiting for our car, I entertained the children, putting pennies on the

> "It was revealed to them that they were serving not themselves but you, in the things that have now been announced to you through those who preached the good news to you by the Holy Spirit sent from heaven, things into which angels long to look."
>
> 1 Peter 1:12 (ESV)

railroad tracks and waiting for the train to pass so we could collect what we thought looked like a souvenir coin. It doesn't matter where we are; if we have God in our hearts, we are not abandoned or lost.

After our car had been fixed, we got rid of most of the items to minimize the weight and continued the trip. Noticing that the car wasn't going to make it to California, we rented a U-Haul to finish our trip. I knew God was in charge of our trip because even though Ruben had a hard time getting the car into the U-Haul by himself, somehow he managed to wheel it in from a very difficult and dangerous position. When we finally arrived in Fresno, California, the first thing I did was to kiss the ground I was standing on, thanking my Father God for he had been our strength throughout the entire trip just as we had asked of him. As I write this story and because Ruben is no longer with us, I want his family to know how thankful I am he took time off from his busy work to accompany us in our long and difficult trip to California, setting an example and meaning to the scripture *"Love thy neighbor like yourself." Romans 13:9*

A new challenge had begun for me in California, but I knew I could count on God Almighty again and again who has always been here for me. My friend and I helped each other by sharing an apartment until I was able to get my own. When I started teaching, I moved into my own apartment with all the necessary things for my family. This was a blessing for both of us because we needed more space for our children; and I was also sending for my brother to care for my children when they came home after school, and I was still at work. The blessings continued as one day, my brother was waiting for me at the Fresno Airport, singing and whistling while the breeze blew

> **"When the Son of Man comes in his glory, and all the angels with him, then he will sit on his glorious throne.**
>
> **Mathew 25:31 (ESV)**

his red hair from side to side, showing me his happiness; he was ready to start a new life as a special uncle to my children. Even though he was quite young, he quickly learned to cook and do chores he ended up doing most of the time since I was working two to three jobs during that time. These responsibilities and his good grades while attending college helped him to achieve success at work and with his own family, who constantly appreciate his love and kindness. God rewards the pure in heart like my brother, who has always been there for me when I need him.

On my own and as a single parent, my life was quite complex because now I was not only responsible for my two children but for my brother as well. I knew there was no time for pain or tears, and that I needed to continue working hard if I were to reach my goals. On a daily basis, I would pray—strengthening my faith in God and waiting for his will to be done.

It seemed that time was moving fast and my prayers answered sooner than I thought because within a few months in California, I had an apartment, a full-time job, plus the opportunity of a part time that I could depend on to help manage my finances in times of difficulties. I was very thankful to my Father God for helping me endure long hours of studies, which is an important key to being a successful citizen as a part of any community. I know that without his guidance, I could not have met my goals. I see my education as a result of God's will first and my effort and strong desire to succeed second. He is an awesome father who watches his children even before birth.

As I continued relying on my faith in God, I continued meeting my goals as a professional and fulfilling all my responsibilities as a mother. While working as a resource teacher, I was also blessed with a part-time job for Staff Development. It was a wonderful experience

> **behold, he put no trust in his servants;
> and his angels he charged with folly**
>
> **Job 4:18**

to teach educators as well as learning from them during their class presentations. I always looked forward to teaching these classes because as teachers we were all committed to learning. There were many nights that I came home very late and tired after teaching, but my heart was content and full of joy because that day I had been able to share my knowledge with students and teachers while providing for my family. I will never forget the laughter and happiness on teachers' faces one day when right before lunch, I decided to give them happy faces as a reward for their work. I believe rewards are very important for children as well as for adults. It feels good when someone tells you, "You are doing a great job," or "Your improvement is moving you toward excellence." Just a note saying, "Good Job" makes a difference in people.

As I continued working and enjoying God's blessings one day, I decided that it was time for me to purchase a home for my family. When I saw a home for sale, I fell in love with this home because it had everything necessary for us to be comfortable including a swimming pool to keep my children busy while exercising during the summer. When I asked for the price which I couldn't afford at that time, I kept praying and telling God how much I liked that house, to please give it to me if it was his will.

I believe God gives us the desire of our heart if what we want is part of his plan and on his own time. Since I couldn't afford it, I kept praying and asking God for just any home. A year later I noticed that the same home was still for sale, and because the price had gone down, I was able to purchase it as if God had saved it for my family as one of his blessings to us.

The story that I am about to tell you is a recount of my encounter with identical angels. It happened in my son's bedroom one Sunday morning while I was struggling with the back pain I had learned to

> "Ask it will be given to you, seek and you will find, knock and the door will be open to you."
>
> Mathew 7:7

live with. I am writing this story for the honor and glory of God and telling you about my heavenly experience beyond your imagination. I have prayed and asked God for wisdom and words that will take you inside my home and bedroom where the angels appeared, giving you the opportunity to see how our prayers are answered because of God's love for us. I have also asked God that I don't add or take away any word or letter that may interfere with the veracity of this story and to bless each person reading this book and believing that angels are real; and if it's God will, they can be seen too. They are God's messengers, ready to help us even though we can't see them. I also believe they come with a purpose—in times of trouble, happiness, or during our special prayer.

If only one person is touched in a very special way by reading this book, then I have met my goal for writing it. It has not been easy for me—writing this book—because I am not a writer, but a simple person telling a true story that needed to be shared with others as it is one beautiful experience showing God's greatness on earth. Today as you read my story, I would like to let you know that, yes, angels are real because I was in their presence; I saw them and if you are in trouble, you are not alone—just ask God to help you and to send angels too.

I have had many beautiful experiences in my life that I treasure in my heart—like the birth of my child ren, my first job, and when I moved into my first home—but nothing can be compared to the experience of

having real angels appear before me in broad daylight at the footstep of my bed and talking to me in their own language.

If your only experience with angels has been through books or paintings, and nobody you know of has seen angels, then you probably wonder if they really are the way they have been depicted.

> **for thou hast made him a little lower than the angels, and hast crowned him with glory and honor.**
>
> Psalms 8:5

Through this experience, I had the opportunity not only of seeing how some angels in heaven look like, but I also learned how important it is to ask God in prayer for the things I desire.

This encounter with angels **changed my life, brought me closer to God, and made me aware that angels, look** like you and me—but with the ability to do things that you and I cannot do. I was amazed by the fact that the angels that came to my house were able to come and go without making any noise other than the sound they made with their wings as they were leaving.

There were many times when getting ready for bed, I knew in my heart angels were next to me because even though I couldn't see them; I could feel their presence. I have continued praying and asking God to please send me angels if it's his will. Even though this encounter with angels happened twenty-three years ago, this vision is as clear to me as if it had just happened yesterday. For many years, I have wanted to share this beautiful experience with the world, but I have always wondered if people would believe me. Also, not being sure if a vision of this magnitude was to be kept in my heart or to be shared with others, I had to pray and wait for the right time to write this book.

After my retirement, I felt the urge to write this book and share this story with others. It is going to be difficult for everyone who reads this book to believe and understand my encounter with angels if they have not been through the same experience. However, I must not depart from this earth without letting the world know about this vision for the honor and glory of God; believing it will strengthen the faith of believers and will encourage future generations to put God first in their lives.

> "See, I am sending an angel before you, to guard you on the way "With all my heart I praise you, Lord In the presence of angels, I sing your praises."
>
> Psalm 138:1 Contemporary English Version

What I saw

As a single parent, every day was a different challenge trying to raise my children, working more than one job, and, at the same time, learning to live with a constant back pain. Every day I would pray, asking God for strength and wisdom. I would also ask Him for angels to help me achieve my daily goals.

In 1988, one Sunday morning and the week before Mother's Day at about 9:30 a.m., while living in Fresno, California, I received a gift from heaven that I will never forget. It was a beautiful morning with a cold breeze, and the sun was already shining through the bright white clouds announcing a beautiful, sunny day.

My kids had been sleeping in my bed because I had the custom of keeping them with me at night for safety. I crept out of bed quietly; and like in most mornings, I woke up with a backache.

After having coffee and checking on the kids that were still sleeping, I walked to my son, Joel's bedroom, to lie down on his bed because he had a waterbed with a motor that kept the water warm, which was very helpful for my back.

> "And he will send out his angels with a loud trumpet call, and they will gather his elect from the four winds, from onke end of heaven to the other."
>
> Mathew 24:31 (ESV)

Joel's room was a normal boy's room painted in white with a hard wood floor and decorated with boats and beach scenes which reminded me of Puerto Rico. I still remember the lamp on top of his dresser made out of burlap with a wooden boat at the bottom. The lamp had a small light bulb that gave a soft yellow light, changing the color of the white walls and bringing out the beach scenes of the few paintings around the room, creating an atmosphere of a cool evening when the sun is going down as the night approaches. The small dresser was to the right of the bed against the small wall between the closet and the window. The closet was located at the end of the room with a wooden top to keep toys and store unused items. There was an area between the bed and the closet where the angels stood that morning.

The room had two big windows—one facing the street with a constant display of cars and from the other where one could see a beautiful view of the sky.

This window, which was located behind the headboard, was very special because lying in bed one could see clouds formed in a magnificent view of shapes and designs that can only be created by heavenly hands—God's powerful hand through lightning and thunder during a rainy day, stars during a bright night keeping its distance from each other in obedience to God, or a flock of birds crossing the sky in perfect position as if they were in training following the leader or guided by a special hand. The big window added one more painting to my son's room in which canvas was constantly being reused by the changes in weather and time of the day as a remembrance that God is the greatest artist of all.

My favorite part of the room was his waterbed located in the center of the room in a wooden frame. Even though it was a very

> "See that you do not despise one these little ones, For I tell you that in heaven their angels always see the face of my Father who is in heaven."
>
> Mathew 18:10 (ESV)

inexpensive bed, for me, it was a wonderful tool to massage and diminish my pain. Lying on my back, I could feel the motion of the water as if I was floating on top of the ocean waves and being carried away. This always gave me a sense of peace, helping me to relax my body and mind while having an open communication with God.

As I lay down that Sunday morning on my son's waterbed to relax my back, I closed my eyes and started thinking about all the things I had planned to do that day. After a few minutes, I opened my eyes and, to my surprise, I had identical, beautiful big angels standing in prayer and a small one kneeling and floating closer to me. The first question I asked myself was, *"Is it that I'm dying?"*

At that moment, I realized that my body was totally stiff, and my eyes were wide open, but I couldn't blink or move. I knew that I was perfectly fine because I wasn't feeling any pain or discomfort, nor was I scared. I was feeling calm, peaceful, and at the same time trying to understand what was happening while carefully observing them.

The first thing I noticed was they were two identical angels, so I carefully looked at them to make sure I wasn't confused. As they stood there long enough for me to observe them, I had the time to confirm that they were indeed identical angels because I carefully counted four wings. I couldn't understand why they were identical, but it was very clear to me that there were two angels in front of me who were exactly the same.

The identical angels' faces were small round and very white. Both faces were completely soft and shiny as if they had been covered with white powder and very small particles of silver glitter. They looked quite young with smooth skin and probably between fifteen or twenty years old. Their eyes were closed, and their heads were tilted down a little bit. Their eyelashes were normal size in length but

> "Just so, I tell you, there is joy before the angels of God over one sinner who repents."
>
> Luke 15:10 (ESV)

thin. Their noses were small, and their small mouths were closed. Their eyebrows were normal in size but thin. They had both hands folded in prayer pose right under their chins, and I could see their short nails. They seemed to be tall or at least taller than I am. Their wings caught my attention because they were immense in proportion to their bodies. The wings didn't have feathers like birds, but I did notice what looked like little veins. The wings were of some white texture that was smooth like cotton balls and with some silver particles that look like glitter.

Both angels had neck-length black hair, parted in the middle, and with stiff curls curved back away from their faces over the ears. The hair was very stiff, and I could see a little bit of white dust on top of their heads to the right of the parted hair.

Their gowns were loose, straight, and very white. It seemed like they were made out of white cotton with long sleeves which were a little bit wide at the end. I cannot describe their feet to you because they were standing at the foot of the bed, and I could only see them to just below their waist.

The little angel was in a kneeling position, floating close to my knees as I'm lying down straight on the bed. The small angel had very little wings that kept him floating; but for some reason, even though he was the closest one to me, I couldn't distinguish his facial characteristics and for that reason I cannot describe him to you as I am describing the identical angels.

It gave me the impression that the little angel's mission was to communicate the message given to me by the identical angels behind him. I talk more about the identical angels since they were the ones that looked very real to me, and I am still able to describe. . . Every time I heard a word or words coming from the little angel, a light would light up in the big angels' chest but not in the little angel's

> **"For this very night there stood before me an angel of the God to whom I belong and whom I worship;"**
>
> Acts 27:23 (ESV)

chest; the reason for that was I knew the identical angels were the ones doing the talking even though they were not moving their lips. I noticed their chest and gowns were transparent because every time a word came out of the little angel, I could clearly see a bright yellow light in the identical angels' chest. They spoke in an unfamiliar language, but the last words they said as they were leaving were, "And, and, and." I couldn't understand why their last words were in English, but the last words I heard were exactly *and* three times.

Just before leaving, I heard the noise you hear when someone blows air but loud enough, for I could hear it or maybe the sound of an Airplane taking off but not as loud since we were in the bedroom. As they left, I saw part of a wing passing right over my face; but my body was still stiff, and all I was able to do was look at it. They left the room flying over my body through the window behind the bed, and I have never seen them again, not even in my dreams.

> **English Standard Version**
> For there will never cease to be poor in the land.
> Therefore I command you, "You shall open wide your hand
> to your brother, to the needy and to the poor, in your land."
>
> Deuteronomy 15:11

After the Angels left

After the angels left, I noticed that I was able to move my body; and immediately got out of bed and went directly to the window behind the bed, hoping to see them flying toward the sky or disappearing among the clouds. After a few seconds and because I didn't see them, I thought they were probably somewhere in the house, and started to look in every possible corner of the house. When I couldn't find them, I realized that I had seen them leave and overpowered by the beautiful experience I just had and not knowing what to do or whom to tell who would believe me, I sat down for a few minutes to think about what to do. The first thing that came to my mind was to contact the local newspaper, the Fresno Bee, to share my story with them but there was no answer.

Since I had the need to tell someone I called my friend, Connie. I knew that my friend Connie would believe me and would help me find an answer for a vision of this magnitude because she knew me

> "An angel of the Lord appeared to the woman and said to her, "Though you are barren and have had no children, yet you will conceive and bear a son."
>
> **Judge 13:3 New American Bible**

well. We both tried to figure out why angels had come to see me and what was the meaning of the message; but as hard as we tried, it is impossible to analyze things that you do not understand and that are too complex for a human being to comprehend.

> "The righteous care for the needs of the animals but the kindest acts of the wicked are cruel."
>
> Proverbs 12:10 (NIV)

An experience with my dog

That Sunday, after I finished my conversation with Connie, I went to check on my white poodle. The dog was very special to me because it was given to me by a very dear friend. I went outside to the patio where I usually played with him, and to my surprise, he wasn't there. I called him a couple of times without a response, but because he used to go around the neighborhood every time he found the gate opened, I wasn't worried. When I realized that my dog wasn't home, I got in my car and went around the block, carefully looking in each of my neighbors' front yards, hoping to see him. I was almost at the end of the street and very scared because, at that point I thought I had lost him, but I spotted him at my neighbor's front yard hurt and bleeding profusely. I picked him up and rushed to the veterinarian, hoping to save his life. When the veterinarian saw the dog, he informed me my dog had a fifty-fifty chance of living and that he was going to need surgery and a couple of days at the hospital, but he couldn't promise me the dog was going to live. I was devastated thinking that my dog wasn't going to make it and that he was going to be gone forever. At that moment, I got closer to the dog; and by looking into his eyes, I was able to communicate with him,

> *"Delight yourself in the Lord and he will give you the desires of your heart"*
>
> Psalm 37:4 (NASB)

and somehow I knew in my heart that he wanted to live. Sure of my decision, I went ahead and approved his surgery and the necessary care at the pet hospital asking God to please take care of my dog and not to let him die.

After a few days, my dog was home recuperating, and I was glad I had made the right decision because he had survived. I still remember the vet's question, "Do you want me to go ahead with the surgery or put him to sleep?" My answer was clear and calm, "Please go ahead with the surgery, Doctor."

I was very thankful to my Father God, for he had given me my dog back. God watches over everything he has created, and we are given animals to love them, care for them, and to handle their well-being since they cannot take care of themselves. When I see my dog, Sandy sick, I gently touch her head and pray for her, believing God heals the animals because he loves all his creation.

> "Then the devil left him, and behold, angels came and were ministering to him."
>
> Mathew 4:11 (ESV)

Why was I chosen

Being chosen to participate in a special event or to receive an award is always a wonderful experience especially if one has worked very hard to receive that specific reward and was looking forward to being chosen. However, it has been very difficult for me to understand why I had been chosen by God to see angels because even though I love God with all my heart and I am constantly praising and thanking him for all his blessings, I feel there are other people who are more worthy of receiving this vision. When I saw the angels, I had been attending a small Christian church for a few years. I could feel the presence of our Father God in all the services and activities of the church. My favorite part of the service has always been when I hear the speaking of tongues as the entire church unite in a powerful prayer after God's message for that day or when the pastor's wife, leads us in singing Christian songs that edify my spirit and makes me feel closer to God. It is at this time when I present my petitions before the Lord, talking to him like I talk to a friend without being heard by the congregation that cohesively and loudly praises the Lord with all their hearts. I always remember the glow on my children's faces as we sang "This Little Light of Mine" on the way home after each service.

> "My God sent his angel and shut the lions, mouths, and they have not harmed me, because I was found blameless before him; and also before you, O KING, I have done no harm."
>
> Daniel 6:22 (ESV)

When I received the visit of the angels, I was living a very busy life, working and taking care of my family. I wasn't fasting or in prayer at the mountains but always thanking him for my blessings and constantly praying with faith that God, in his time, would heal my back. I knew he was the one giving me the strength to accomplish my daily tasks.

Not a single day passes without me thinking about this vision, and I am always asking myself the same question, "Why was I chosen to see angels?" It will be wonderful to find an answer for an experience like this one. One night while watching a program, I heard that people with near-death experiences have celestial visions. I don't know if this vision is related to that information or not as God is the one deciding

who receives a vision and the reason, but I have included in my book some of my experiences as a possible connection. Again and again, I thank God for this beautiful visit of angels.

When I was at the hospital giving birth to my daughter, I remember that when I opened my eyes after the surgery, my husband was in tears; and I couldn't understand why he was sad if that was a moment of joy and happiness. The day I was released from the hospital ,as we were passing by the nurse's counter, I heard when one nurse told the other, "Is that the lady that was brought back to life with the defibrillator? I immediately turned around and looked to see if there was another patient leaving the hospital next to me and seeing that I was the only one passing by their counter I realized that I had died, but God had allowed the doctors to bring me back to life. My husband didn't say a word, but I remembered that when I got to the hospital that day, the doctors were concerned and rushed me to the surgery room. I also remember what I thought was a dream,

> "Then the woman came and told her husband, "A man of God came to me, and his appearance was like the appearance of the angel of God, very awesome. I did not ask him where he was from, and he did not tell me his name."
>
> Judges 13:26 (ESV))

seeing myself above the bed where I was lying during the surgery and looking down, I could see a body with doctors and nurses working on it. I had no idea whose body that was, and I wasn't feeling pain or fear. I cannot tell you that I saw a tunnel or lights because I didn't, but I do know I felt calm. God, because of his love, had given me one more opportunity to be here on earth and to raise my children that otherwise would have been left without a mother.

I will continue looking for an answer to my vision; however, it is beyond my comprehension, and I will probably never find an answer unless God gives me a message with an explanation if it's his will. Since I was constantly asking God to send me angels and because the Bible teaches us *"Ask and you shall receive," Matthew 7:7,* the only answer for this vision that I can think of is that God answered my prayer by sending real angels from heaven to share with others—for his glory and for the reason he only knows. One day, I asked my son-in-law, who serves God with all his heart and is a man of wisdom, "Mijo, Why do you think I saw these angels?" His answer was, "Tata, God heals whom he wants and blesses whom he wants for reasons that we don't know."

A few years after the apparition of angels, I was referred to a surgeon who made a very small incision on my back; and since then, I have the normal aches and pains like everyone experiences but the back pain I called "a trial" was lifted from my body for the glory of God when a doctor did a simple procedure completing with it, my healing. After that surgery, I have developed strength in my entire body; and started doing yard work, cleaning, and lifting quite heavy objects. Climbing on top of my house to pick figs became an easy task as I do it almost every day during the fig season. God is in charge of

> **Of the Angels he says; "He makes his angels winds, and his ministers a flame of fire"**
>
> **Hebrews 1:7 (ESV)**

our doctors and uses them to complete our healing when necessary. I know my surgery was a work of art, and I will always be thankful to my Father God for answering my prayer in a special way and to my doctor for his dedication to medicine. I always ask God to help me enter the kingdom of heaven so that I can relive what I saw on earth.

I have continued praying; asking him to send angels but always thanking him first for everything he has given me. I start my prayer by thanking God for my family, my job, one more day on earth, each star of the universe, each flower, each leaf on the tree, the water, the air that I breathe, the birds, the animals in the oceans, and for all the things he created in the universe which cannot be seen. I will never stop thanking my Father God for his son, Jesus Christ, who set an example of humility and love for us to follow in order to enter the kingdom of heaven as the time is getting closer.

I would like to finish this chapter with the following words: ***"Share your blessings God gave you with others in need."*** I always keep these words present in my heart because if each one of us shares a little bit of what we have with others who are sick, hungry, or homeless—not only are we helping others in need to have a little bit but also our Father God in heaven rejoices as he sees us sharing the blessings we have because he gave them to us.

> "Then I lifted my eyes and saw, and behold two women coming forward! The wind was in their wings. They had wings like the wings of a stork, and they lifted up the basket between earth and heaven.
>
> Zechariah 5:9 (ESV)

Wings in Joel's picture

When God gave me the opportunity to work at a small country school in California, I was also blessed with Sylvia, a godly woman with whom I had the joy to share the responsibilities of this job. I knew that teaming with a godly person was going to be one more key element for us to do an outstanding job and to be a role model for others. We always enjoyed our job working as a team because we both shared things in common not only as professionals but also as women of faith. Our positions gave us the opportunity to meet the needs of our students and assist the teachers while developing a Christian friendship that evolved through prayer and sharing God's greatness during lunch time. I still remember her thanking God for he had given us a job that brought joy to our heart through the children and because we could work as a team following our Christian principles. Since she was already working for the school when I was hired, she kindly shared her small office, giving me an area next to a window to put my desk and my pictures. I immediately used it to organize my

> **Whosoever therefore shall be ashamed of me and of my words in this adulterous and sinful generation; of him also shall the Son of man be ashamed, when he cometh in the glory of his Father with the holy angels.**
>
> **Mark 8:38**

desk and computer, displaying my favorite pictures including one of my son's, Joel, who was in the army and stationed in Saudi Arabia.

It was 1995 when my son, Joel, was deployed to Saudi Arabia on a six-month mission. After celebrating his departure, I folded the big poster of encouragement I had hung up on the kitchen's wall and asked God to watch over him, sending angels to be with him. I was proud to see my son serve his country, but I was also concerned for his safety. Laying hands on Joel's picture every day, I would ask God to please send angels to watch over my son and to keep him in his hands.

Because I did this every day, I had every detail of his picture already imprinted in my mind. After a few months of prayer, one Thursday morning and a week before Christmas vacation, I opened my office door; and to my surprise, I found two small wings—one on each side of my son's picture perfectly defined including little veins that one could think an artist came and drew them the night before. I showed the picture to my friends and everyone who came to my office that day to share God's love for us. For people who had seen the picture many times, it was clear that the wings were around my son. Two days after, my son came to the United States from being stationed in Dhahran, Saudi Arabia; there was an explosion at the Kobar Towers where he had been staying, and it was evident to me that God had sent angels to watch over him because he had been protected from the hands of the enemy by not being there when the explosion occurred. I know that a parent's prayers are answered

> **New American Bible Version** "I Jesus, sent my angel to give you this testimony for the churches. I am the root and offspring of David, the bright morning star."
>
> **Revelation 22:16**

and if we keep our children in constant prayer, God will send angels to watch over them, keeping them safe. The best advice I can give a parent is to pray day and night for their children, believing that your prayer, has been answered. Never stop praying for your children because a prayer is the best gift a parent can give to a child as he or she was the best gift given to them from our Father God in heaven.

- *For when they shall rise from the dead, they neither marry, nor are given in marriage; but are as the angels which are in heaven. Mark 12:25*
- *And then shall he send his angels, and shall gather together his elect from the four winds, from the uttermost part of the earth to the uttermost part of heaven. Mark 13:27*

Sammy's Angel

It is said that children can see things that adults might not be able to see because of their innocence and the purity of their hearts. I have been blessed with five grandchildren that came into my life, bringing me the joy and happiness grandparents experience through grandchildren. My first grandchild, Sammy, moved to Los Angeles with his family and every year, we look forward to seeing each other during his summer vacation to spend quality time and continue building memories I want him to share one day with his family. When he comes to visit me, our days are full of laughter while having a good time telling stories, cooking, or looking at the stars.

It is a wonderful experience when Sammy shares his computer savviness with me, a gift that he has had since he was a little boy. When grandparents give the grandchildren the opportunity to be their teacher, we are not only promoting their self-esteem, but also giving them the opportunity to expand their knowledge while building a stronger relationship that is so important for both grandparents

> "He drove out the man, and at the east of the garden of Eden he placed the cherubim and a flaming sword that turned every way to guard the way to the tree of life."
>
> **Genesis 3:24 (ESV)**

and grandchildren. When children are with adults, it is important to teach them as many things as possible by involving them in a lot of activities and encouraging them to participate so they can become independent and successful citizens in our complex society. Sammy was about ten years old when he came to spend his summer vacation with me, and I still remember the happiness on his face and in my heart as he ran through the front door gathering his pieces of clothes as they fell off his unzipped backpack.

One Sunday night, after a fun day of activities we call "making memories," I went to bed early and left him playing games downstairs with my nephew. I told him to come to bed before midnight, and it was about 11:30 p.m. when Sammy was on the way to his bed. As he was passing by the kitchen which is connected to the sunken family room, a bright light caught his attention. When he turned his face to see where the light was coming from, he was astonished to see that the bright, sparkling light was coming down from the vaulted ceiling, lighting the face of an angel that was kneeling in prayer between the family room and the kitchen. After looking at the angel, he ran upstairs and while shaking me, he started calling my name and saying, "Tata, Tata come downstairs, there is an angel praying in your family room." I could hear him, but I was so tired and sleepy that I could hardly understand what he was trying to tell me. Being that Sammy was so persistent and insisting for me to go downstairs and because he kept saying, "Nobody believes me," I opened my eyes and seeing the expression on his face, I knew that he had seen something and I needed to find out. I jumped out of bed, and as we are both running downstairs Sammy kept telling me, "Tata, you are not going to see the angel because you didn't get up when I told you to."

> "And to grant relief to you who are afflicted as well as to us, when the Lord Jesus is revealed from heaven with his mighty angels."
>
> 2 Thessalonians 1:7 (ESV)

When we got downstairs, the angel was already gone and I could see on his face that he was disappointed because he was hoping to share this experience with me. He looked at me and pointed to the area where he had seen the angel, continued saying, "See, Tata, I told you to get up and you didn't." I asked him a little bit about the angel he had seen. He talked about the bright light with sparkles that came down from the high vaulted ceiling. I told him we would talk more about the angel the next day at dinner time because it was late and I had to work the next day.

The next morning, I went to work and during lunch, as usual, we as a group of teachers got together to eat in my classroom. I told the teachers that Sammy had seen an angel in my family room, but I would give them the description the following day because I was tired and told Sammy to tell me about the angel he saw the next day when I was rested and the time to attentively listen about his experience and the angel he had seen. That same day and during dinnertime, Sammy said the angel had shoulder-length curly black hair and was kneeling with hands folded in prayer. He said the angel was wearing a wrinkled white gown and had folded big wings. The light with what he called little stars was coming down on the angel from the vaulted ceiling, the reason for which he was able to see the angel. When I asked Sammy if the angel looked at him, he answered, "No, Tata. I was not seen because the angel's eyes were closed. I looked at the light to see what it was and when I saw the angel, I ran upstairs to tell you."

The following day, as we are getting ready to eat lunch, I told the teachers that I wanted to give them the description of the angel Sammy had seen, and at that moment, Maria Dorado, the second-

> And he said unto him, "Truly, truly, I say to you, you will see heaven opened, and the angels of God ascending and descending on the Son of Man."
>
> John 1:51 (ESV)

grade teacher who was expecting her second child, looked at me saying she had seen an angel in her dream the night before and she would like to describe the angel she saw in her dream first. When Maria finished describing the angel, I was amazed to see that for some reason God had shown her the same angel Sammy had seen in our family room.

The description of the angel seen by Maria in her dream was the same exact description given by Sammy during our conversation at dinnertime, reason for which I have no doubt in my mind that Maria's vision of the angel in her dream was God's confirmation to me that Sammy indeed saw the angel; and probably because I hesitated to get up right away, he showed Maria the angel as a confirmation of his appearance. Until this day, Sammy talks about the angel he saw and how he thinks I didn't see the angel for not going downstairs when he told me so. If this vision was not for me but for Sammy, I am very happy to see that like me, he had the opportunity to see an angel while here on earth. Maria, the second-grade teacher, still remembers her dream. Like we want God to listen to us when we talk to him, one must listen to our children because God can be talking to us through them; and if we are not good listeners, we might miss a blessing sent to us through our children. Always remember what Jesus said, ***"Let the children come to me because theirs is the kingdom of heaven." Matthew 19:1***

> - I looked again and heard the voices of many angels who surrounded the throne and the living creatures and the elders. They were countless in numbers. Revelations 5:11 (NABV)
> - *"This is how it will be at the end of the age. The angels will come and separate the wicked from the righteous"* Mathew 13:49 (NIV)

An angel in school

Hello, my name is Gabrielle Maria, and I am ten years old. My favorite pastime is to spend time with my family going to church, praying, and reading my Bible. I also enjoy playing softball and participating in my school performances. I am a sixth-grade student at a Christian school in Fresno, California. First Church Christian Academy is a school with a small student population and with a curriculum that includes God's word on a daily basis. I have been attending this school since I was in pre-k. It has helped me to learn my reading, writing, and math; more than anything, it has strengthened my relationship with God. Every time I enter the school, I am entering a place that makes me feel peaceful; I can feel God's love coming from all the teachers and students. For me, everything in my school is fun whether I am in a classroom, cooking with Mr. Vanburen, or doing activities with Ms. Price.

My Tata has been writing a book about angels based on an experience she had in my bedroom when my mom was about my age

> "A stream of fire issued and came out from before him; a thousand thousands served him, and ten thousand times ten thousands stood before him; the court sat in judgment, and the books were opened."
>
> **Daniel 7:10 (ESV)**

and living in the same house I am living in now. I was excited to hear about Tata's story, and I started to wonder if I could see an angel too.

Quietly in my room, I started praying every night that God would allow me to see angels.

One Friday, September 3, 2010, I woke up at 6:45 a.m. as I usually do. I got ready for school, had my breakfast, and headed for school like I normally do. I met my friends in the cafeteria waiting for the bell to ring, and by 8:15 a.m. I was in Mr. Sanchez's class. I went through all of my classes following my daily schedule, but I wasn't prepared for what I was about to see before the end of the day.

It was about one o'clock in the afternoon when I was going to my Bible class. After getting to the fireside room for my Bible class, I noticed that I had left my Bible assignment back in my homeroom. As I started to walk back to get the page I needed for my class, I passed by our school playground and saw something out of the corner of my eye that caught my attention. When I took a closer look, I noticed that what I was seeing was an angel sitting on the hoop with both legs bent and hugged knees with arms while looking at two other kids go by. I was so astonished that my feet grinded against the sand, which caused us both to look up at each other. As I turned around, the angel gasped in amazement to see me. I hurried back through the gate to the fireside room. I got back to class and plumped myself down on the seat waiting for further instructions. As I turned around to look at the door, I saw the angel again standing there, smiling and waving at me. Because the entire class was quietly working on an assignment, I didn't say anything not only because I thought they would never believe me, but because that would make people think that I was looking at a stranger, that would have caused a lockdown.

> "And there appeared to him an angel of the Lord standing on the right side of the altar of incense. And Zechariah was troubled when he saw him, and fear fell upon him. But the angel said to him, "Do not be afraid, Zechariah, for your prayers has been heard, and your wife Elizabeth will bear you a son, and you shall call his name John. And you will have joy and gladness, and many will rejoice at his birth, for he will be great before the Lord. And he will not drink wine or strong drink, and he will be filled with the Holy Spirit, even from his mother's womb...."
>
> Luke 1:11-20 (ESV)

Our next elective was music which takes place at the chapel in the sanctuary. We were onstage practicing for the performance for the next day when I saw the angel come in and sit down next to one of the parents who was picking up her kid. The angel sat down and started waving at the parent, trying to get noticed, but the parent didn't notice. I saw when the angel got up and went to the corner and followed Mr. V to the back of the sanctuary. I kept looking and studying the angel. The angel's skin was olive in color, had long curly black hair, and had blue eyes. The gown was plain white with elbow-length sleeves. The gown had a golden rope over the left shoulder coming down to the waist and tied around on the right side. The angel had beautiful big white wings sprinkled with silver dust that were close together; barefooted, short and looked like my age, which was ten. As I kept practicing, I noticed the angel was at the end of the stage to my right copying every step I did. Since I was paying too much attention to the angel and not to Ms. Price, I got corrected by my teacher. After apologizing to my teacher, I turned to look, and at that moment, the angel left flying through the wall and has never been seen again.

That Friday, my Tata went to pick me up at school and asked me how my day had been. I told her that I had seen an angel at school. My Tata was amazed to know that I had seen an angel because she had been praying God to allow us, her family, to have an experience

> **Psalms 68:17 The chariots of God are twenty thousand, even thousands of angels: the Lord is among them, as in Sinai, in the holy place. Bless the Lord all you angels mighty in strength and attentive obedient to every command.**
>
> **Psalm 34:7 NAB**

like hers. The fact that I saw an angel makes my Tata wonder how many people in this world have seen angels but have not shared this experience with other people, or if there is a special reason angels are visiting our family.

After seeing this angel, I now understand more about angels because I have personally seen one. I thank God for my experience, and I hope that God will allow me to see greater things.

- *American Standard Bible Version "And Jacob went on his way, and the angels of God met him" Genesis 32:1 (ASBV)*
- *But of that day and* that *hour knoweth no man, no, not the angels which are in heaven, neither the Son, but the Father. Mathew 13:32 (ASBV)*

My son-in-law converses with angels

My Son in law has been serving God and constantly praising and thanking him for all his blessings and for guiding his family. As the head of household, he makes sure that on a daily basis, God is first in everything his family does. I was amazed to see how he taught his daughters to read by reading a chapter of the Bible every day with them as they repeated after him.

One night, when he was soundly asleep in his bedroom, he was suddenly awakened by two men standing next to him by his bedside. He said he was not scared and felt at peace with the two strange men standing next to his bedside. He asked the men how they had gotten into the house since the house alarm was activated and did not sound. One of the men said, "Follow us." The next thing he knew, he found himself in the living room with the men. It was very strange to him because he said they did not walk to the living room but rather just suddenly appeared there. He asked them again how they got into the house, and one of them pointed up at the ceiling. He just looked at them with a confused look and repeatedly told them that why didn't his house alarm sound. He then asked them as one of the men was pointing up at the ceiling, "What do you mean from up there?" The

> **Then I saw another mighty angel coming down from heaven, wrapped in a cloud, with a rainbow over his head, and his face was like the sun, and his legs like pillars of fire. He had a little scroll open in his hand. And he set his right foot on the sea and his left foot on the land, and called out with a loud voice, like a lion roaring. When he called out, the seven thunders sounded. And when the seven thunders had sounded, I was about to write, but I heard a voice from heaven saying, "Seal up what the seven thunders have said, and do not write it down." And the angel whom I saw standing on the sea and on the land raised his right hand to heaven...**

next thing he knew, he and the two men were up in his attic. While in the attic, one of the men continued to point up. He looked up and found a twelve-by-twelve hole in his roof. He gazed intently through the opening and it went straight into the heavens. At that instant, he knew that these were no ordinary men, but angels sent from God. He knew that God had shown him that his angels were keeping watch over his household. Instantly, he began to turn to the angels to tell them he knew they were angels, but he did not see them any longer next to him in the attic. At that moment, my daughter began shaking him.

He was awakened in his bed at the sound of his house alarm blaring in the night. My daughter was yelling at him that someone must have been breaking into the house. He jumped out of bed, and as he ran through the house looking for a burglar and the sound of the alarm blaring, he could only think about the angels. As he completed a look around the house, he determined that there were no obvious signs of a burglar and shut off the alarm. He told his wife that everything was fine and to go back to sleep. As he placed his head back on his pillow, he could not help but giggle and say to God, "That was no burglar. You were just reminding me of what you had just shown me."

The next day, his mom came to his house because for the past week they had been remodeling his house so that he could have a room to himself. He called it his prayer room because that is where he would go to seek God and to prepare his sermons because he preaches at times at his

> **In just the same way I tell you there will be rejoicing among the angels of God over one sinner who repents.**
>
> **Luke 15:10 New American Bible**

church. When he told his mother about his experience the night before, she insisted that he should go to the attic. He laughed and told her, "Mom, what would I be looking for if I go up there?" His mother told him she did not know, but God would show him when he got up there. After several minutes of debating whether he should go or not, he finally went. The entrance to the attic is in his daughter's room in the closet. As he walked toward his daughter's room, he kept thinking, "What am I going to be looking for?" He moved his daughter's belongings and made a clearance so he could climb into the attic. He moved the ceiling cover, and as he climbed into the attic, he yelled to his mother, "You are never going to believe this!" He sat in the attic in amazement looking up at the roof. He recently had work done on his house by the city's airport. Since he lives in the path that airplanes fly over to land at the airport, the airport replaced all of his windows and doors (sound proofing them). The airport also sent workers up into the attic to place wood in front of all the vents in the roof so that the sound from the planes would reflect off the wood. As he stared up, he noticed that exact area where the angel had pointed in the roof, the twelve-by-twelve wood was loose and hanging down by two nails. He also realized that this opening was also directly over the room where I had told him that angels stood in 1988 when I lived there. He just sat there in awe looking at the attic. As he stared at the wood hanging down, he just kept telling God how awesome he was.

I thank God for these experiences with angels given to my family because now they have become part of my story. Because these experiences happened in my family while I was writing this book, I also see it as God telling me what needs to be in this book that has been difficult to write because I cannot add or take away a word that would interfere with the veracity of the book, as I said at the beginning.

> "Then I looked, and I heard around the throne and the living creatures and the elders the voice of many angels, numbering myriads of myriads and thousands of thousands, saying with a loud voice, "Worthy is the Lamb who was slain, to receive power and wealth and wisdom and might and honor and glory and blessing!"
>
> **Revelation 5:11-12**

Two days later, after this experience, he woke up in the morning as usual people do and began to prepare his daughters' school lunches. As he stood in the kitchen, he heard his middle child, Gabby, yelling. He ran to their bedroom, and as he entered the room, he saw his daughter, Gabby, standing next to her bed holding a burnt blanket. Immediately, he knew the blanket had fallen onto the lamp that his girls keep on the ground next to their bed. This lamp burns very hot and he had told himself about a week prior that he needed to remove this lamp from their room because he thought it was very dangerous. He grabbed the blanket and noticed that the corner had caught fire in the night and burnt. His daughter, Gabby, said, "Daddy, we could have been burned alive last night." He just looked at his girls and said, "We need to thank God for keeping you safe." They all told God thank you for keeping them safe. He took them to school and as he was driving back home, he could only think how all three of his daughters were in that bed. Even though his daughters have their own beds, they choose to sleep together. When he returned home, he went directly to his daughters' room and grabbed the burnt blanket. He held the blanket up in the air toward heaven and said, "There is no reason this blanket should not have continued to catch fire and burn my daughters." He prostrated himself on her bed and wept very loud. He wept for what seemed an hour. He wept and wept, thanking God for sending his angels to blow the fire out. He knew that God had saved all three of his daughters from burning to death that night. I know in my heart the angels he saw days prior were watching over his family as they said.

> "Then I saw another angel flying directly overhead, with an eternal gospel to proclaim to those who dwell on earth, to every nation and tribe and language and people."
>
> Revelation 14:6

The nurse at Community Hospital

When one is ill in the hospital, we depend on doctors and nurses to improve our health—a job that is not easy because it requires physical and mental strength. I have always been thankful and appreciative of nurses because my experience with them in the hospital has always been positive. When you have a loved one in the hospital, you depend on the patience, knowledge, and dedication of each nurse and doctor to bring that family member home in good health.

In 2004, my husband had surgery at the Fresno Community Hospital in Fresno, California. I was there almost every day from 4:00 p.m. until 9:00 p.m. giving him support and companionship while checking on his health progress. In one of the visits, I noticed that the nurses were quite busy like always; however that specific night, they seemed to be busier than the other nights I had been visiting the hospital. It gave me the impression that there were probably more patients in need of their services than the night before, and when Alfred asked me if I could give him a bath, I saw it as an opportunity

> **The crowd there heard it and said it was thunder, but other said, "An angel has spoken to him."**
>
> **John 12:29 New American Bible**

to help the nurses by giving him a bath that would help him relax and fall asleep. As I am finishing by washing his feet, I noticed that he was falling asleep and in a soft voice thanked me and told me to go home that he wanted to sleep. It was about 9:00 p.m. when I left the room walking towards the elevator, which was at the end of a long hall with offices on both sides of the hall. While passing by the nurses' counter, I could hear how busy they were with patients calling, requesting different services, which made me think how blessed we are that nurses one day decided to prepare themselves for this demanding job that not only requires them to work different shifts, but to be constantly aware of each patient's medications and health status. *Acts 20:35 in all things I have shown you that by working hard in this way we must help the weak and remember the words of the Lord Jesus how he said, "It's more blessed to give than to receive."*

As I'm leaving that night, I said, "Good night," informing them that I was leaving and continued my peaceful walk to the elevator through the long and quiet hall, feeling a sense of fulfillment and joy in my heart which comes when doing a good deed for the benefit of another human being. I was probably halfway between the elevator and the nurses' counter when I heard loud footsteps rushing behind me. Knowing how busy the nurses were that night, all that came to my mind was that they had one more emergency to take care of, and I kept walking since I knew hospitals emergencies are constantly happening day and night. As I am getting closer to the end of the hall, a nurse with shoulder-length black hair and with a stethoscope around her neck caught up with me saying that she was sorry if she had scared me; but she was the person running fast behind me, trying to catch up with me because she had seen something wide and bright over my head, and she was wondering what kind of hat I was wearing.

> **And it came to pass, as the angels were gone away from them into heaven, the shepherds said one to another, Let us now go even unto Bethlehem, and see this thing which is come to pass, which the Lord hath made known unto us. Luke 2:15 (KJV)**

Shocked for what she had said, all that came to my mind to say was, "Oh! Those are my angels." When we got to the elevator, I didn't ask her any questions about what she had just seen because I was still in shock, and I wasn't even sure if she was a real person or if she was an angel talking to me since I had seen angels before. As we got down, we both got out of the elevator, and I stood there watching her walk away to see if she was indeed a nurse or if I had seen an angel. After seeing her join a group of nurses and talking to them, I realized that she was a nurse and God had given her a heavenly vision to share with me because of his love. However, that was my thinking at that moment, we never know why one person has a vision because it is God who decides whom to give a vision and for the reason he does it. Everyone's job is important, and we all have responsibilities in our jobs as we all have a mission on earth to fulfill. Every time I visit a hospital and I see doctors and nurses coming and going, I think of them as special people on earth for all patients because whether family members are there or not, they are the ones responsible for the prompt recuperation of that patient which also includes feeding, bathing, and comforting. In many occasions, they are also the last ones to pray or be there for the ones near death—or—for those near their deathbed.

Two years ago, God gave me the opportunity to visit a Christian church in Puerto Rico. The pastor's wife who has the gift of prophecy called me to the altar and while praying for me said, "God sent you a message in an elevator." It is hard for me to understand the message God sent me through the nurse, but one thing clear to me is that when you have the will and the desire to help, if you do it with all your heart one can feel the presence of God who is there with us at all times and can see when we choose to do what is right. I always

> **And it came to pass, as the angels were gone away from them into heaven, the shepherds said one to another, Let us now go even unto Bethlehem, and see this thing which is come to pass, which the Lord hath made known unto us. Luke 2:15 (KJV)**

thought this message was for the nurse, but God makes sure we get the messages he sends to us. The best thing one can do for a sick person whether at home or a hospital is to wash and massage his/her feet. It is the best way to help the person relax and fall asleep

> "Be strong and of a good courage, fear not, nor be afraid of them: for the Lord thy God, he {it is} that doth go with thee; he will not fall thee, nor forsake thee."
>
> Deuteronomy 31:6 (KJV)

Living with the presence of God in our lives

We all live a life with the presence of God as we are all his creation. Living with the presence of God has been a blessing in my life because in his presence, I have been able to accomplish what I wanted and needed in my life. With my life constantly changing and with the daily demands and responsibilities toward my job and family, the presence of God in my life has always given me the peace, strength, and wisdom necessary to make important decisions.

Knowing that he is everywhere, I know he is here for me and all I have to do is call upon him. Until this day and for the rest of my years he may grant me to live on earth, I see him as my constant companion who never lets me down because he is part of my daily life. Living with God in my heart has been essential for me to meet my goals without giving up when faced with difficult tasks. When a challenge approaches my life, I take it one step at a time, believing that the outcome is the result of what my Father God has in his plans

> "Fear thou not; for I {am} with thee: be not dismayed; for I {am} thy God: I will strengthen thee; yea, I will help thee; yea, I will uphold thee with the right hand of my righteous."
>
> Isaiah 41:40 (KJV)

for me, because ,being he is present in my daily life, he knows exactly what I need.

I pray to God for his will to be done and I thank him for answering my prayers according to his will.

One thing that I enjoy doing is looking at God's presence in my surroundings. I think it is wonderful when I go outside and look at a piece of the sky with beautiful clouds and stars. Whether I am poor or rich, I enjoy the same beautiful sky as everyone else. I might not be able to afford a mansion, but I have a beautiful piece of sky that is free for me to look at. Taking time to look at a flower in my backyard and thinking how this flower came to be: the form, the color, all the petals connected together in a perfect form; looking at a small fruit that is barely starting to grow and comparing it to a full-grown fruit—a pine tree with thousands of needles perfectly in place with each branch or a lemon tree next to the pine tree getting ready to give us sustenance—shows me the presence of God in everything and because I am part of everything he created, he lives within me. I acknowledge his presence in everything I do and say by thanking him.

Touching a rock or a tree, I ask God for strength when my body is weak or to anoint me with the first raindrop that falls on my head. With the rays of the majestic sun, I ask him to touch my eyes and with the water to heal my body and mind. It is because of his presence that I am not alone and that I am who I am and because of his presence, I have been blessed.

I have learned that by asking God for guidance in everything I want to do is like having celestial key opening doors for me on earth. I strongly believe that completing a simple task like buying a pair of shoes is directed by God if I call upon him when I am standing right

> "I was in the city of Joppa praying: and in a trance I saw a vision, A certain vessel descend, as it had been a great sheet, let down from heaven by four corners; and it came even to me:"
>
> Acts 11:5 (KJV)

there in front of rack after rack not knowing which pair of shoes will be better or more comfortable for me.

When I feel disappointed because after praying, waiting, and praying again and the answer is not what I expected, I just ask God to guide me so I can understand his decision. I always remember that he has all the power over heaven and earth to make things happen, but because nobody knows me better than he does, I trust in him—accepting and thanking him for his decision even when is not the one I was expecting.

Living with the presence of God in my life is like looking at things through a magnifying glass which makes small things bigger and clearer, showing details that otherwise one cannot see.

While living in Connecticut, one night during a snowstorm I got lost and ended up at a deserted park. My car got stuck in the snow, and I panicked because I had my children with me in the car. I sat there not knowing what to do, but God's presence was evident. I immediately, opened the trunk of my car looking for something that would help me and saw a carton box which I opened, putting one piece of carton under each tire. When I started the car it spun in circles a few times but I didn't lose control and was able to get back on the road. I thank God for this wonderful idea and for helping me to continue my trip safely. Knowing that God is perfect, I am very careful in everything I do and say as he is the one watching my steps. "Thank you, Father God, for your constant presence in my life and for answering my prayers.

> **Remember your creator in the days of your youth before the days of trouble come and the years approach when you will say,**
> **"I find no pleasure in them."**
>
> **Ecclesiastes 12:1 NIB Version**

As you finish reading this book, I pray for God to send angels over you and your family, to answer your prayers, and to heal your body if you are sick. If you have been touched by this book, I would like to know about it since this book has only been written for the honor and glory of God. **What I have written in this book is what I saw, and I have asked God to help me recount it exactly the way it happened.**

"Heavenly Father, in this book I have written and illustrated the vision you sent me. My job is finished, and the book is in your hands."

> "Surely he will save you from the fowlers' snare and from the deadly pestilence."
>
> Psalm 91:3 (NIV)
>
> "And in the last days it shall be, God declares, that i will pour out my Spirit on all flesh, and your sons and your daughters shall prophesy, and your young men shall see visions, and your old men shall dream dreams."
>
> Acts 2:17 (ESV)

After my retirement

My retirement has been very rewarding, busy, and with many new experiences. However It doesn't matter how old or young we are, trials are always following us through our entire lives. In my life, I have gone through a lot of difficult trials but with my strong faith in God who makes the impossible " possible", I always find a way to solve situations not only for me but for family members as well. I strongly believe our Father God guides me to do what I need to do, when I ask him for help in order to overcome a difficult situation.

    Now that I am retired I continue to pray under the stars, thanking God for his blessings and taking pictures of the night sky.

    Many times after praying until very late at night and when I go to bed, I receive celestial visions of things that eventually happen.

> "I saw in the night visions, and behold, with the clouds of heaven there came one like a son of man, and he came to the Ancient of of Days and was presented before him."
>
> Daniel 7:13 (ESV)

It is like my soul leaves my body and I start seen things that I know are not from this earth. When I get up the next day, I always go to my calendar and write time and day God gave the vision and what was it about. In my next book, I will be writing and illustrating each vision I have had for the honor and glory of God. I am going to tell you about a vision I had in January 22, 2020 because I have been impacted by this vision.

On January 22, 2020 and after 2:00 a.m., I went to bed. I saw a blue sky with hardly any clouds and in it a huge word written in white and capital letters that read "**KILL**". **I looked down and I saw a huge area that was devastated. There were no trees, people, or animals. I was worried because all I saw was dirt in a big bare area with small hills. I bent down and I saw a very big round watch which looked like a man's watch. I picked it up and I noticed it was in silver, very heavy, and with black numbers. The time was not clear to me but it was before 12:00. I put it in my pocket and gathered three small stones which was the only thing left on the ground. Suddenly, I was awake and in my bed. I thank you Father God for this vision.**

To my love ones

Dear children, grandchildren, and family

It has taken me almost four years to write this book, and I want to thank you for your words of encouragement and support. I want you to remember that I thank God for the best gift he gave me when both of you were born. I love you with all my heart because you are wonderful children and my blessing on earth. I have written about my personal life because I want the reader to see how putting God first in my life has helped me accomplish my goals in life and overcome difficult situations. Believing that everything in my life is connected, I found it necessary to talk about my personal experiences even though it was painful and difficult to do.

  Because each event written in this book happened just as I have written it and you know me better than anyone else, I want you to keep this book in a safe place and share it with your children and grandchildren, as I believe it will strengthen their faith in God.

  Here are some words of wisdom to keep in your heart as it is the best gift I can give you with this book.

- *Always put God first in your life, believing that he is in control of all his creation. In sickness, teach your mind to control your*

body through prayer, and don't let your body control your mind.
- *Be careful with what you say; you don't want to regret it.*
- *Have faith that things will get better, and always be prepared because after the storm comes the calm, and after the calm, a storm might come.*
- *Share your blessings with others as God shares them with you. What belongs to the earth will stay on earth.*
- *Positivism is an important key toward success. A negative word is like a bouncing ball; it can very easily come back to you*

Very Important ! It is important that you obey the Ten Commandments because they are necessary to help you live a good life and to enter the kingdom of heaven

> *Therefore whoever relaxes one of the least of these commandments and teaches other to do the same will be called least in the kingdom of Heaven, but whoever does them and teaches them will be called great in the kingdom of heaven*
>
> *Mathew 5:19 ES*

"For he shall give his angels charge over thee to keep thee in all thy ways. They shall bear thee up in their hands, lest thou dash thy foot against a stone." —Psalm 91:11-12 King James 2000
Tomie
1 Corinthians 13:2 New American Standard Bible version
"For he shall give his angels charge over thee to keep thee in all thy ways.

1 Corinthians 13:13 English Standard Bible version

"Then the angel I saw standing on the sea and on the land raised his right hand to heaven" Rev: 10:5 New International Bible

"See, I am sending an angel before you, to guard you on the way and bring you to the place I have prepared" Exodus 23:20

*"With all my heart I praise you, Lord
In the presence of angels, I sing your praises." Psalm 138:1 Contemporary English Version*

"Then the angel I saw standing on the sea and on the land raised his right hand to heaven" Rev: 10:5 New International Bible

*"See, I am sending an angel before you, to guard you on the way
"With all my heart I praise you, Lord
In the presence of angels, I sing your praises." Psalm 138:1 Contemporary English Version*

*Joshua 1:9 New International Version
Have I not commanded you? Be strong and courageous. Do not be terrified; do not be discourage, for the Lord your God will be with you wherever you go"*

"An angel of the Lord appeared to the woman and said to her, "Though you are barren and have had no children, yet you will conceive and bear a son." Judge 13:3 New American Bible

In just the same way I tell you there will be rejoicing among the angels of God over one sinner who repents. Luke 15:10
New American Bible
The crowd there heard it and said it was thunder, but other said, "An angel has spoken to him." John 12:29 New American Bible

And to strengthen him an angel from heaven appeared to him. Luke 22:43 NAB

Bless the Lord all you angels mighty in strength and attentive obedient to every command. Psalm 34:7 NAB

The angel of the Lord, who encamps with them delivers all who fear God. Psalm 34:7 NAB

Exodus 23:20 NAB
"See, I am sending an angel before you, to guard you on the way and bring you to the place I have prepared.

Luke 1:13 NAB
But the angel said to him," Do not be afraid, Zechariah, because your prayer had been heard. Your wife Elizabeth will bear you a son, and you shall name him John.

Psalm 103:20 NAB
Bless the LORD, all you angels, mighty in strength and attentive, Obedient to every command
Zechariah 1:11 NAB Version
And they answered the angel of the LORD who was standing among the myrtle trees and said, "We have patrolled the earth; see, the whole earth is tranquil and at rest"

1 Samuel 29:10 NAB Version
*So the first thing tomorrow, you and your lord's servants,
who came with you, go to the place I picked out for you. Do not
decide to take umbrage at this; you are as acceptable to me
as an angel of God. But make an early morning start,
as soon as it grows light, and be on your way."*

Deuteronomy 15:11 English Standard Version
*For there will never cease to be poor in the land.
Therefore I command you, "You shall open wide your hand
to your brother, to the needy and to the poor, in your land."*

Matthew 28:2 NABRE Version
*And behold there was a great earthquake;
for an angel of the Lord descended from heaven,
approached, rolled back the stone, and sat upon it.*

Luke 1:26 NAB Version
In the sixth month the angel Gabriel was sent from God
to a town of Galilee called Nazareth

2 Kings 1:15 NAB Version
*Then the angel of the LORD said to Elijah,
"Go down with him; you need not be afraid of him."*

Genesis 32:1 American Standard Version
"And Jacob went on his way, and the angels of God met him."

Psalm 91:11 New American Bible
For God commands the angels to guard you in all your ways.

Psalm 37:4 New American Standard Bible
"Delight yourself in the Lord and he will give you
the desires of your heart"

Judges 2:1 New American Bible Version
An angel of the LORD went up from Gilgal to Bochim and said,
"It was I who brought you up from Egypt and led you into
the land which I promised on oath to your fathers. I said that
I would never break my covenant with you,

1 Timothy 2:2-6 English Standard Version
First of all, I urge that supplications, prayers, intercessions
and thanksgiving be made for all people, for kings and all who
are in high positions, that we might lead a peaceful
and quiet life, godly and dignified in every way
Revelation 22:16 New American Bible Version
"I Jesus, sent my angel to give you this testimony for the churches.
I am the root and offspring of David, the bright morning star."

Revelation 10:1 New American Standard Bible Version
Then I saw another mighty angel come down from heaven wrapped in
a cloud, with a halo around his head; his face was like
the sun and his feet were like pillars of fire.

Then I said, "What are these my Lord?" The angel who talked with
me said to me, "I will show you what they are." Zechariah 1:9

Rev. 5:11 NAB Version
I looked again and heard the voices of many angels
who surrounded the throne and the living creatures
and the elders. They were countless in numbers.

Genesis 32:1 American Standard Bible Version
"And Jacob went on his way, and the angels of God met him"

Matthew 13:49 New International Version
"This is how it will be at the end of the age. The angels will come and separate the wicked from the righteous"

Remember your creator in the days of your youth before the days of trouble come and the years approach when you will say, "I find no pleasure in them." Ecclesiastes 12:1 New International Version

- *The crowd there heard it and said it was thunder, but other said, "An angel has spoken to him." John 12:29 New American Bible*

- *"See, I am sending an angel before you, to guard you on the way and bring you to the place I have prepared." Exodus 23:20 NAB*
- *Psalm 91:11 New American Bible For God commands the angels to guard you in all your ways.*
- *And to strengthen him an angel from heaven appeared to him. Luke 22:43 NAB*
- *The angel of the Lord, who encamps with them delivers all who fear God. Psalm 34:7 NAB*
- *Psalm 103:20 NAB* Bless the LORD, all you angels, mighty in strength and attentive, Obedient to every command
- *And they answered the angel of the LORD who was standing among the myrtle trees and said, "We have patrolled the earth; see, the whole earth is tranquil and at rest" Zechariah 1:11 NAB Version*
- *And behold there was a great earthquake; for an angel of the Lord descended from heaven, approached, rolled back the stone, and sat upon it. Matthew 28:2*
- *Matthew 25:41 Then shall he say also unto them on the left hand, Depart from me, ye cursed, into everlasting fire, prepared for the devil and his angels:*

- *Luke 1:26 NAB Version* In the sixth month the angel Gabriel was sent from God to a town of Galilee called Nazareth
- *Then the angel of the LORD said to Elijah, "Go down with him; you need not be afraid of him." 2 Kings1:15 NAB Version*
- *So the first thing tomorrow, you and your lord's servants, who came with you, go to the place I picked out for you. Do not decide to take umbrage at this; you are as acceptable to me as an angel of God. But make an early morning start, as soon as it grows light, and be on your way." 1 Samuel 29;10 NAB version*

- *An angel of the LORD went up from Gilgal to Bochim and said, "It was I who brought you up from Egypt and led you into the land which I promised on oath to your fathers. I said that I would never break my covenant with you, Judges 2:1 NAB Version*
- *Thinkest thou that I cannot now pray to my Father, and he shall presently give me more than twelve legions of angels? Matthew 26:53*
- *And he was there in the wilderness forty days, tempted of Satan; and was with the wild beasts; and the angels ministered unto him. Mark 1:13*

www.ingramcontent.com/pod-product-compliance
Lightning Source LLC
LaVergne TN
LVHW011737060526
838200LV00051B/3205